Edward Arber, Thomas Dekker

The seven deadly sins of London, drawn in seven several coaches, through the seven several gates of the city

Edward Arber, Thomas Dekker

The seven deadly sins of London, drawn in seven several coaches, through the seven several gates of the city

ISBN/EAN: 9783744741583

Printed in Europe, USA, Canada, Australia, Japan

Cover: Foto ©ninafisch / pixelio.de

More available books at **www.hansebooks.com**

The English Scholar's Library etc.

No. 7.

The Seven deadly Sins of London &c.

[October] 1606.

The English Scholar's Library of
Old and Modern Works.

THOMAS DECKER.

The Seven deadly Sins of London

drawn in seven several coaches, through
the seven several gates of the
City ; bringing the plague
with them.

[October] 1606.

Edited by EDWARD ARBER, F.S.A., etc.

LECTURER IN ENGLISH LITERATURE ETC.,
UNIVERSITY COLLEGE, LONDON.

SOUTHGATE LONDON, N.

15 April, 1879.

No. 7.

CONTENTS.

BIBLIOGRAPHY

ISSUE IN THE AUTHOR'S LIFETIME.
As a separate publication.

1. [Oct.] 1606. 4to. See title at *p.* xv.

The registration at Stationers' Hall is as follows :

6 𝔒𝔠𝔱𝔬𝔟𝔯𝔦𝔰 [1606.]

Nathaniel Butter. Entred for his copie vnder th[e h]andes of master HARTWELL and master Warden **white** A Book called *The Seuen deadly synnes of London, drawen in 7 seuerall coaches throughe the 7 gates of the City.* **vj**d **.w.**

Transcript &c. iii. 330. Ed. 1876.

⁂ It is stated in the copy (10,452) in the Grenville Collection in the British Museum, that this is " the rarest of Dekker's pieces."

ISSUES SINCE HIS DEATH.
A. *As a separate publication.*

2. 1866. London. 4to. Privately printed (edition of Forty copies only). *Illustrations of Old English Literature.* Vol. ii. Edited by J. PAYNE COLLIER, F.S.A. · *The Seven deadly Sins &c.* is one of the distinct reproductions comprising this Series.

Mr. COLLIER says, " We are aware of nothing precisely like it in our language, either for invention, or for accuracy and vivacity of description."

3. 15 April, 1879. Southgate, London, 8vo. The present impression.

B. *With other works.*
None known.

INTRODUCTION.

ULL of striking invention and imagery conceived in as religious a spirit as that of JOHN BUNYAN ; written in a strong yet quaint and bedecked style, which appears to be an engrafting of the punning of JAMES's reign on the Euphuism of Elizabeth's time ; so rich in words, similes, and allusions of the day as to be capable of almost indefinite annotation ; replete with so many graphic touches of life and character : this intensely earnest Apologue—at once a sermon, a pageant, and a satire—dashed off in a week by one who was both a Poet and a Dramatist, will amply repay the close attention of the student of the Golden Age of our Literature.

II.

F the framework and outward form of this old Interlude of *Iniquity*, the abstract given at *pp*. vi. and vii. will here suffice. Let us see "what a number of colours are here grounded, to paint out" by a Londoner (*p*. 9), the sights and sounds of ordinary life in the metropolis in the fourth year of JAMES I. : sights and sounds which we can well suppose were as well noted by the observant eye of SHAKESPEARE, during his late residence of nearly twenty years in town, as then by his younger and lesser compeer DECKER.

Here is a short sketch of London by day.

In euery street, carts and Coaches make such a thundring as if the world ranne vpon wheeles : at euerie corner, men, women, and children meete in such shoales, that postes are sette vp of purpose to strengthen the houses, least with iustling one another they should shoulder them downe. Besides, hammers are beating in one place, Tubs hooping in another, Pots clincking in a third, water-tankards running at tilt in a fourth : heere are Porters sweating vnder burdens, there Marchants-men bearing bags of money, Chapmen (as if they were at Leape frog) skippe out of one shop into another :

Tradesmen (as if they were dauncing Galliards) are lusty at legges and neuer stand still: all are as busie as countrie Atturneyes at an Assises. *p.* 31.

To which may be added an afternoon performance, say, at the Blackfriars Theatre.

The Players prayed for his comming, they lost nothing by it, the comming in of tenne Embassadors was neuer so sweete to them, as this our sinne was; their houses smoakt euerye after noone with Stinkards, who were so glewed together in crowdes with the Steames of strong breath, that when they came foorth, their faces lookt as if they had beene perboylde: And his *Comicall Tearme-time* they hoped for, at the least all the summer, because tis given out that *Sloth* himselfe will come, and sit in the two-pennie galleries amongst the Gentlemen, and see their *Knaueries* and their pastimes. *p.* 32.

And finally the arrival of candle light at nightfall.

No sooner was he aduaunced vp into the moste famous Streetes, but a number of shops for ioy beganne to shut in: Mercers rolde vp their Silkes and Veluets: the Goldsmithes drew backe their Plate, and all the Citty lookt like a priuate Play-house, when the windowes are clapt downe, as if some *Nocturnal*, or dismall *Tragedy* were presently to be acted before all the *Trades-men*. But *Caualiero Candle-light* came for no such solemnities: No he had other Crackers in hand to which hee wacht but his houre to giue fire. Scarce was his entrance blown abroad, but the Bankrupt, the Fellon, and all that owed any mony, and for feare of arrests, or Iustices warrants, had like so many Snayles kept their houses ouer their heads al the day before, began now to creep out of their shels, and to stalke vp and down the streets as vprightly, and with as proud a gate as if they meant to knock against the starres with the crownes of their heads. *p.* 25.

III.

AT the same time, mere description of life was not primarily intended by the writer. It is a half-religious, half-dramatic invective against the iniquity of the day that was unpunishable by law, such as DANIEL DE FOE might have written; and on account of which the writer prognosticates a renewal of the recent plague of 1603. The various classes that are satirized in it, are specified in the *Contents* at *p*. v. Let us see his warning to the best of them, the clergy.

There is yet one more, whome I would not heare to *Cry Guilty*, because (of all others) I would not haue them slothfull. O you that speak the language of *Angels*, and should indeed be *Angels* amongst vs, you that haue offices aboue those of Kinges, that haue warrant to commaund Princes, and controle them, if they do amisse : you that are Stewards ouer the Kings house of heauen, and lye heere as Embassadors about the greatest State-matters in the world : what a dishonour were it to your places, if it should bee kuowne that you are Sloathfull ? you are sworne labourers, to worke in a Vineyard, which if you dresse not carefully, if you cut it nót artificially, if you vnderprop it not wisely when you see it laden, if you gather not the fruites in it, when they bee ripe, but suffer them to drope downe, and bee eaten vp by Swine. O what a deere account are you to make him that must giue you your hire ? you are the Beames of the Sun that must ripen the grapes of the Vine, and if you shine not cleerely, he will eclipse you for euer : your tongues are the instruments that must cut off rancke and idle Sprigs, to make the bearing-braunches to spred, and vnlesse you keepe them sharpe and be euer pruning with them, he will cast you by, and you shall be eaten vp with rust. The Church is a garden and you must weede it : it is a Fountaine, and you must keepe it cleere : it is her Husbands Jewell, and you must pollish it : it is his best belooued, and you must keepe her chast.

Many Merchants hath this Cittie to her Sonnes, of al which you are the most noble, you trafficke onely for mens Soules, sending them to the Land of *Promise*, and to the heauenly *Ierusalem*, and receiuing from thence (in *Exchange*) the richest Commoditie in the world, your owne saluation. O therefore bee not you Slothfull : for if being chosen Pilots, you Sleepe, and so sticke vpon Rockes, you hazard your owne shipwracke more then theirs that venture with you. *pp.* 33, 34.

I V.

THE *Induction to the Book* and those numerous apostrophes in London, as *Thou, thy country's darling ! Thou leader of so great a kingdom ! Fair Troy-novant !* show how much the mind of the writer was imbued with the style of the old Hebrew prophets; and how sure he was that that style would find a response in the hearts of his readers.

There is also the following quaint description of the human body, with which we must here conclude.

Man (doubtlesse) was not created to bee an idle fellow, for then he should bee Gods *Vagabond*: he was made for other purpose then to be euer eating as swine: euer sleeping as *Dormise*: euer dumb as fishes in the Sea, or euer prating to no purpose, as birdes of the ayre: he was not set in this *Vniuersall Orchard* to stand still as a *Tree*, and so to bee cut downe, but to be cut downe if he should stand still.

And to haue him remember this, he carries certaine *Watches* with *Larums* about him, that are euer striking: for all the *Enginous Wheeles* of the *Soule* are continually going: though the body lye neuer so fast bownde in Slumbers, the imagination runnes too and fro, the phantasie flyes round about, the vitall spirits walke vp and downe, yea the very pulses show activitie, and with their hammers are still beating, so that euen in his very dreames it is whispered in his eare that hee must bee dooing something. If hee had not these prompters at his elbowe ye euerie member of his body (if it could speake woulde chide him) if they were put to no vse, considering what noble workmanship is bestowed.

For man no sooner gets vpon his legges, but they are made so that either hee may run or goe: when he is weary, they can giue him ease by standing still, if he will not stand, the *Knees* serue like Hindges to bow vp and downe, and to let him kneele. His armes haue artificiall cordes and stringes, which shorten or flye out of their length at pleasure: They winde about the bodye like a siluer *Girdle*, and being held out before, are weapons to defend it.

At the end of the armes are two beautiful *Mathematicall* Instruments, with fiue seuerall motions in each of them, and thirtie other mouing *Engines*, by which they stirre both.

His head likewise standes vpon three *Skrewes*, the one is directly forward to teach him *Prouidence*, the other two are on eather side one, to arme him with *Circumspection*: How busie are both the eyes, to keepe danger from him. *pp*. 30, 31.

THE
Seuen Deadly Sinnes

of London :

Drawn in seuen seuerall Coaches,
Through the seuen seuerall Gates of the
Citie

Bringing the Plague with them.

Opus septem Dierum.

Tho : Dekker.

At London
Printed by *E.A.* for *Nathaniel Butter,* and are to bee sold
at his shop neere Saint Austens gate.
1606.

To the Worshipfull and very worthy Gentleman *Henry Fermor* Esquire, Clarke of the Peace for the
Countie of Middlesex.

Am sory (deare Sir) that in a time (so abundant with wit) I shold send vnto you no better fruit then the sins of a City : but they are not common, (for they were neuer gathered till this yeare) and therefore I send them for the *Rarity*: Yet now I remember my selfe, they are not the *Sinnes* of a Citie, but onely the picture of them. And a *Drollerie* (or Dutch peece of *Lantskop*) may sometimes breed in the beholders eye, as much delectation, as the best and most curious master-peece excellent in that Art. Bookes being sent abroad after they are begotten into the world, as *This of mine is,* are in the nature of *Orphans*; But being receiued into a *Gardianship* (as I make no doubt but this shall) they come into the happie state of adopted children. That office must now be yours, and you neede not bee ashamed of it, for Kings haue beene glad to doe them honour, that haue bestowed such a neuer-dying honour vppon them. The benefite you shall receiue, is this, that you see the building vp of a tombe (in your life time) wherein you are sure so to lie, as that you cannot bee forgotten; and you read that very Epitaph that shal stand ouer you, which by no *Enuie* can bee defaced, nor by any time worne out. I haue made choise of you alone, to bee the *onely Patron* to these my labours: by which word (*onely*) I chalenge to my selfe a kinde of *Dignitie*: for there hath beene a *Generation* of a sort of strange fellowes (and I thinke the race is not yet eaten out) who when a Booke (of theire owne) hath bin borne in the lawfull Matrimonie of Learning, and Industrie, haue basely compeld it either like a bastard, to call a great many father (and to goe vnder all their names) or else (like a common fellow at a Sessions) to put himselfe (as the tearme is) vpon twelue godfathers. In which case (contrarie to all law) the Foreman is most dishonoured. That art of *Skeldring* I studie not, I stand vpon stronger Bases. The current of a mans Reputation, being diuided into so manie Riuolets must needes grow weake. If you giue intertainment to this in your best affection, you will

binde me (one day) to heighten your name, when by some more worthy *Columne* (by me to be erected) I shall consecrate that and your selfe to an euerlasting and sacred Memorie.

Most affectionately desirous to be yours.

Tho. Dekker.

Reader,

IT is as ordinarie a custome (for vs that are Bookish) to haue a bout with thee, after wee haue done with a Patron, as for Schollers (in the noble Science) to play at the woodden Rapier and Dagger at the ende of a Maisters prize. In doing which we know not vpon what Speeding points wee runne, for you (that are Readers) are the most desperate and fowlest players in the world, you will strike when a mans backe is toward you, and kill him (if you could for shame) when he lies vnder your feete. You are able (if you haue the tokens of deadly Ignorance, and Boldnes at one time vpon you) to breede more infection on in *Pauls Church-yard*, then all the bodies that were buried there in the Plague-time, if they had beene left still aboue ground. You stand somtimes at a Stationers stal, looking scuruily (like Mules champing vpon Thistles) on the face of a new Booke bee it neuer so worthy : and goe (as il fauouredly) mewing away : But what get you by it ? The Booke-seller euer after when you passe by, pinnes on your backes the badge of fooles to make you be laught to scorne, or of sillie Carpers to make you be pittied : *Conradus Gesner* neuer writ of the nature of such strange beasts as you are : for where as we call you *Lectores*, Readers, you turne your selues into *Lictores*, Executioners, and tormenters. I wold not haue him that writes better than I, to Reade this, nor him that cannot doe so well, to Raile, or if hee cannot chuse but Raile, let him doe it to my face : otherwise (to me being absent) it is done cowardly : for *Leonem mortuum mordent etian Catuli* : Cats dare scratch Lions by the face when they lie dead, and none but Colliers will threaten a Lord Maior when they are farre enough from the Cittie. I haue laide no blockes in thy way : if thou findest Strawes, (*Vade vale.*) *caue ne titubes.*

The names of the Actors in this
old Enterlude of Iniquitie.

1 *Politike Bankeruptisme.*

2 *Lying.*

3 *Candle-light.*

4 *Sloth.*

5 *Apishnesse.*

6 *Shauing.*

7 *Crueltie.*

Seuen may easily play this, but not without a Diuell.

The Induction to the

Booke.

I Finde it written in that Booke where no vntruthes can be read : in that Booke whose leaues shall out-last sheetes of brasse, and whose lynes leade to eternity : yea euen in that Booke that was pend b*y* the best Author of the best wisedome, allowed by a Deity, licensed by the Ómnipotent, and published (in all Languages to all Nations) by the greatest, truest, and onely Diuine, thus I find it written, that for Sinne, Angels were throwne out of heauen ; for Sinne, the first man that euer was made, was made an outcast : he was driuen out of his liuing that was left vnto him by his Creator : It was a goodlier liuing, than the Inheritance of Princes : he lost Paradice by it (he lost his house of pleasure :) hee lost *Eden* by it, a Garden, where Winter could neuer haue nipt him with cold, nor Summer haue scorcht him with heate. He had there all fruits growing to delight his taste, all flowers flourishing to allure his eye, all Birds singing to content his eare ; he had more than he could desire : yet because he desired more than was fit for him, he lost all. For Sinne, all those buildings which that greate Worke-master of the world had in sixe dayes raysed, were swallowed at the first by waters, and shall at last be consumed in fire. How many families hath this *Leuiathan* deuoured ?

2 *

how many Cities ? how many Kingdoms ? Let vs awhile leaue Kingdomes, and enter into Cities. *Sodom* and *Gomorrah* were burnt to the ground with brimstone that dropt in flakes from heauen : a hot and dreadfull vengeance. *Ierusalem* hath not a stone left vpon another of her first glorious foundation : a heauy and fearefull downefall. *Ierusalem*, that was Gods owne dwelling house ; the Schoole where those Hebrew Lectures, which he himselfe read, were taught ; the very Nursery where the Prince of Heauen was brought vp ; that *Ierusalem*, whose Rulers were Princes, and whose Citizens were like the sonnes of Kings : whose Temples were paued with gold, and whose houses stood like rowes of tall Cedars ; that *Ierusalem* is now a dezert ; It is vnhallowed, and vntrodden : no Monument is left to shew it was a City, but only the memoriall of the Iewes hard-hartednes, in making away their Sauiour : It is now a place for barbarous Turks, and poore despised Grecians ; it is rather now (for the abominations committed in it) no place at all.

Let vs hoyst vp more Sayles, and lanch into other Seas, till wee come in ken of our owne Countrey. *Antwerp* (the eldest daughter of *Brabant*) hath falne in her pride, the Citties of rich *Burgundy* in theyr greatnes. Those seuenteene Dutch Virgins of *Belgia*, (that had Kingdomes to theyr dowries, and were worthy to be courted by Nations) are now no more Virgins : the Souldier hath deflowred them, and robd them of theyr Mayden honor : Warre hath still vse of their noble bodyes, and discouereth theyr nakednes like prostituted Strumpets. Famine hath dryed vp the fresh bloud in theyr cheekes, whilst the Pestilence digd vp theyr Fields, and turned them into Graues. Neither haue these punishments bin layd vpon them onely ; for bloud hath bin also drawne of their very next neighbours. *France* lyes yet panting vnder

the blowes which her owne Children haue giuen her. Thirty
yeeres together suffred she her bowels to be torne out by
those that were bred within them : She was full of Princes,
and saw them all lye mangled at her feete : She was full of
people, and saw in one night a hundred thousand massacred
in her streetes : her Kings were eaten vp by Ciuill warres, and
her Subiects by fire and famine. O gallant Monarchy, what hard
fate hadst thou, that when none were left to conquer thee,
thou shouldst triumph ouer thy selfe!   Thou hast Wynes
flowing in thy veynes : but thou madest thy selfe druncke with
thine owne bloud. The English, the Dutch, and the Spanish,
stoode aloofe and gaue ayme, whilst thou shotst arrowes
vpright, that fell vpon thine owne head, and wounded thee
to death.   Wouldst thou (and the rest) know the reason,
why your bones haue bin bruzed with rods of Iron ?   It
was, because you haue risen in Arch-rebellion against the
Supremest Soueraigne : You haue bin Traytors to your Lord,
the King of heauen and earth, and haue armed your selues to
fight against the Holy Land.   Can the father of the world
measure out his loue so vnequally, that one people (like to a
mans yongest child) should be more made of than all the
rest, being more vnruly than the rest ?   O *London*, thou art
great in glory, and enuied for thy greatnes : thy Towers, thy
Temples, and thy Pinnacles stand vpon thy head like borders
of fine gold, thy waters like frindges of siluer hang at the
hemmes of thy garments. Thou art the goodliest of thy
neighbors, but the prowdest ; the welthiest, but the most
wanton. Thou hast all things in thee to make thee fairest,
and all things in thee to make thee foulest ; for thou art
attir'de like a Bride, drawing all that looke vpon thee, to be in
loue with thee, but there is much harlot in thine eyes. Thou
sitst in thy Gates heated with Wines, and in thy Chambers

with lust. What miseries haue of late ouertaken thee ? yet
(like a foole that laughs when hee is putting on fetters) thou
hast bin merry in height of thy misfortunes: She (that for
Qu. Elizabeths almost halfe a hundred of yeres) of thy Nurse became
death. thy Mother, and layd thee in her bosome, whose
head was full of cares for thee, whilst thine slept vpon softer
pillowes than downe. She that wore thee alwayes on her brest
as the richest Iewell in her kingdome, who had continually
her eye vpon thee, and her heart with thee ; whose chaste
hand clothed thy Rulers in Scarlet, and thy Inhabitants in
roabes of peace: euen she was taken from thee, when thou
wert most in feare to lose her: when thou didst tremble (as
at an earth-quake) to thinke that bloud should runne in thy
Channels, that the Canon should make way through thy
Portcullises, and fire rifle thy wealthy houses, then, euen
then wert thou left full of teares, and becamst an Orphan. But
behold, thou hadst not sat many howres on the banks of
King Iames sorrow, but thou hadst a louing Father that adopted
his Coronation. thee to be his owne : thy mourning turnd presently
to gladnes, thy terrors into triumphs. Yet, lest this fulnesse
of ioy should beget in thee a wantonnes, and to try how wisely
thou couldst take vp affliction, Sicknes was sent to breathe
her vnwholsome ayres into thy nosthrils, so that thou, that
wert before the only Gallant and Minion of the world, hadst
in a short time more diseases (then a common Harlot hath)
hanging vpon thee; thou suddenly becamst the by-talke of
neighbors, the scorne and contempt of Nations.

Heere could I make thee weepe thy selfe away into waters,
*A Booke so by calling back those sad and dismall houres,
called, written
by the Author, wherein thou consumedst almost to nothing with
describing the
horror of the shrikes and lamentations, in that *Wonderfull
Playne in
1603, when *yeere,* when these miserable calamities entred in

at thy Gates, slaying 30000. and more as thou *there dyed* heldst them in thine armes, but they are fresh *30573. of that disease.* in thy memory, and the story of them (but halfe read ouer) would strike so coldly to thy heart, and lay such heauy sorrow vpon mine (*Namque animus meminisse horret, luctuque refugit*) that I will not be thine and my owne tormentor with the memory of them. How quickly notwithstanding didst thou forget that beating? The wrath of him that smot[e] thee, was no sooner (in meere pitty of thy stripes) appeased, but howrely (againe) thou wert in the company of euill doers, euen before thou couldst finde leysure to aske him forgiuenes.

Euer since that time hath hee winckt at thy errors, and suffred thee (though now thou art growne old, and lookest very ancient) to goe on still in the follyes of thy youth: he hath ten-fold restor'de thy lost sonnes and daughters, and such sweete, liuely, fresh colours hath hee put vpon thy cheekes, that Kings haue come to behold thee, and Princes *King of* to delight their eyes with thy bewty. None of all *England, and Christierne* these fauours (for all this) can draw thee from thy *King of Denmarke.* wickednes: Graces haue powred downe out of heauen vpon thee, and thou art rich in all things, sauing in goodnes: So that now once againe hath he gone about (and but gone about) to call thee to the dreadfull Barre of his Iudgement. And no maruaile: for whereas other Citties (as glorious as thy selfe,) and other people (as deare vnto him as thine) haue in his indignation bin quite taken from the face of the earth, for some one peculiar Sinne, what hope hast thou to grow vp still in the pride of thy strength, gallantnes and health, hauing seuen deadly and detestable sinnes lying night by night by thy lasciuious sides? O thou beawtifullest daughter of two vnited Monarchies! from thy womb receiued I my being, from thy brests my nourishment; yet giue me leaue to tell thee, that thou hast seuen Diuels within thee, and till they be cleane cast out, the Arrowes of Pestilence will fall vpon thee by day, and the hand of the Inuader strike thee by night. The Sunne will shine, but not be a comfort to thee, and the Moone looke pale with anger, when she giues thee light. Thy Louers will disdayne to court thee: thy Temples will no more send out Diuine oracles: Iustice will take her flight, and dwell else-where; and that Desolation, which now for three yeeres together hath houered round about thee, will at last enter, and turne thy Gardens of pleasure into Church-yards; thy Fields that seru'd thee for walks, into *Golgotha*; and thy hye built houses, into heapes of dead mens Sculs. I call him to witnes, who is all Truth, I call the Cittizens of heauen to witnes, who are all spotlesse, that I slander thee not, in saying thou nourishest seuen Serpents at thy brests, that will destroy thee: let all thy Magistrates and thy officers speake for me; let Strangers that haue but seene thy behauiour, be my Iudges: let all that are gathered vnder thy wings, and those that sleepe in thy bosome, giue their verdict vpon me; yea, try me (as thy brabblings are) by all thy Petit and Graund Iurors, and if I belye thee, let my Country (when I expire) deny me her common blessing, Buriall. Lift vp therefore thy head (thou Mother of so many people :) awaken out of thy dead dangerous slumbers, and with a full and fearelesse eye behold those seuen Monsters, that with extended iawes gape to swallow vp thy memory: for I will into so large a field single euery one of them, that thou and all the world shall see their vglinesse, for by seeing them, thou mayst auoyd them, and by auoyding them, be the happiest and most renowned of Citties.

Politick Bankruptisme,
Or,
The first dayes Triumph of the first Sinne.

T is a custome in all Countries, when great personages are to be entertained, to haue great preparation made for them: and because *London* disdaines to come short of any City, either in Magnificence, State, or expences vpon such an occasion, solemne order was set downe, and seuen seuerall solemne dayes were appointed to receiue these seuen Potentates: for they carry the names of Princes on the earth, and wheresoe're they inhabit, in a short time are they Lords of great Dominions.

The first dayes Triumphs were spent in meeting and conducting *Politick Bankruptisme* into the Freedome: to receiue whom, the Master, the Keepers, and all the Prisoners of *Ludgate* in their best clothes stood most officiously *The maner* readie: for at that Gate, his Deadlinesse challenges *how Bank-* a kind of prerogatiue by the Custome of the Citie, *entertained,* and there loues he most to be let in. The thing *Gate.* they stood vpon, was a Scaffold erected for the purpose stuck round about with a few greene boughes (like an Alehouse booth at a Fayre) and couered with two or three threed-bare Carpets (for prisoners haue no better) to hide the vnhandsomnes of the Carpenters worke: the boughes with the very strong breath that was prest out of the vulgar, withered, and like *Autumnian* leaues dropt to the ground, which made the *Broken Gentleman* to hasten his progresse the more, and the rather, because *Lud* and his two sonnes

stood in a very cold place, waiting for his comming. Being
vnder the gate, there stood one arm'd with an extemporall
speech, to giue him the onset of his welcome : It was not (I
would you should well know) the Clarke of a country parish,
or the Schoolemaster of a corporate towne, yat euery yeere
has a saying to Master Maior, but it was a bird pickt out
of purpose (amongst the *Ludgathians*) that had the basest
and lowest voice, and was able in a Terme time, for a throat,
to giue any prisoner great ods for ye box at the grate : this
Organ pipe was f[o]unde to rore for the rest, who with a hye
sound and glib deliuery, made an *Encomiastick Paradoxicall*
Oration in praise of a prison, prouing, that captiuity was ye
only blessing yat could happen to man, and that a *Politick
Bankrupt* (because he makes himselfe for euer by his owne
wit) is able to liue in any common wealth, and deserues to go
vp the ladder of promotion, when fiue hundred shallowpated
feollowes shall be turnd off. The poore Orator hauing made
vp his mouth, *Bankruptisme* gaue him very good words, and
a handful or two of thanks, vowing he would euer liue in his
debt. At which, all the prisoners rending the ayre with
shouts, the key was turnd, and vp (in state) was he led into
king *Luds* house of *Bondage*, to suruey the building, and
to take possession of ye lodgings ; where he no sooner
entred, but a lusty peale of welcomes was shot out of
Kannes in stead of Canons, and though the powder was
Solamen   exceeding wet, yet off they went thick and three-
miseris socios fold. The day was proclaymed Holiday in all
habuisse
doloris.   the wardes ; euery prisoner swore if he would stay
amongst them, they would take no order about their debts,
because they would lye by it too ; and for that purpose
swarmd about him like Bees about Comfit-makers, and were
drunke, according to all the learned rules of *Drunkennes*, as
Vpsy-Freeze, Crambo, Parmizant, &c. the pimples of this
ranck and full-humord ioy rising thus in their faces, because
they all knew, that though he himselfe was broken, the
linings of his bags were whole ; and though he had no
conscience (but a crackt one) yet he had crownes yat were
sound. None of all these hookes could fasten him to them :
he was (like their clocks) to strike in more places than one,
and though he knew many Citizens hated him, and that if he
were encountred by some of them, it might cost him deere,

yet vnder so good a protection did he go (as he said) because he owed no ill will euen to those that most sought his vndoing; and therefore tooke his leaue of the house, with promise, to be with them, or send to them once euery quarter at the least. So that now, by his wise instructions, if *Misery makes a Puny* were there amongst them, he might learne *men cunning.* more cases, and more quiddits in law within seuen dayes, than he does at his Inne in fourteene moneths.

The *Politician* beeing thus got into the City, caries himself so discreetly, that he steales into the hearts of many: In words, is he circumspect: in lookes, graue: in attire, ciuill: in diet, temperate: in company affable: in *His qualities.* his affaires serious: and so cunningly dooes he lay on these colours, that in the end he is welcome to, and familiar with the best. So that now, there is not any one of all the twelue Companies, in which (at one time or other) there are not those that haue forsaken their owne Hall, to be free of his: yea some of your best Shop-keepers hath he enticed to shut themselues vp from the cares and busines of the world, to liue a priuate life; nay, there is not any great and famous Streete in the City, wherein there hath not (or now doth not) dwell, some one, or other, that hold the points of his Religion. For you must vnderstand, that the Politick Bankrupt is a *Harpy* that lookes smoothly, a *Hyena His disguises.* that enchants subtilly, a Mermaid that sings sweetly, and a *Cameleon*, that can put himselfe into all colours. Sometimes hee's a Puritane, he sweares by nothing but Indeede, or rather does not sweare at all, and wrapping his crafty Serpents body in the cloake of Religion, he does those acts that would become none but a Diuell. Sometimes hee's a Protestant, and deales iustly with all men, till he sees his time, but in the end he turnes Turke. Because you shall beleeue me, I will giue you his length by the Scale, and Anatomize his body from head to foote. Heere it is.

Whether he be a Tradesman, or a Marchant, when he first sets himselfe vp, and seekes to get the world into *His policy.* his hands, (yet not to go out of ye City) or first talks of Countries he neuer saw (vpon the *Change*) he will be sure to keepe his dayes of payments more truly, then Lawyers keepe their Termes, or than Executors keepe the last lawes that the dead inioyned them to, which euen Infidels themselues will not violate : his hand goes to his head, to his meanest customer, (to expresse his humilitie ;) he is vp earlier then a Sarieant, and downe later then a Constable, to proclaime his thrift. By such artificiall wheeles as these, he wind[e]s himselfe vp into the height of rich mens fauors, till he grow rich himselfe, and when he sees that they dare build vpon his credit, knowing the ground to be good, he takes vpon him the condition of an Asse, to any man that will loade him with gold ; and vseth his credit like a Ship freighted with all sorts of Merchandise by ventrous Pilots: for after he hath gotten into his hands so much of other mens goods or money, as will fill him to the vpper deck, away he sayles with it, and politickly runnes himselfe on ground, to make the world beleeue he had sufferd shipwrack. Then flyes he out like an Irish rebell, and keepes aloofe, hiding his head, when he cannot hide his shame : and though he haue fethers on his back puld from sundry birds, yet to himselfe is he more wretched, then ye Cuckoo in winter, that dares not be seene. The troupes of honest Citizens (his creditors) with whom he hath broken league and hath thus defyed, muster themselues together, and proclaime open warre : their bands consist of tall *Yeomen,* that serue on foot, commanded by certaine *Sericants* of their bands, who for leading of men, are knowne to be of more experience then the best Low-country Captaines. In Ambuscado do these lye day and night, to cut off this enemy to the City, if he dare but come downe. But the politick Bankrupt barricadoing his Sconce with double locks, treble dores, inuincible bolts, and pieces of timber 4. or 5. storyes hye, victuals himselfe for a moneth or so; and then in the dead of night, marches vp higher into ye country with bag and baggage; parlies then are summond ; compositions offred ; a truce is sometimes taken for 3. or 4. yeeres ; or (which is more common) a dishonorable peace (seeing no other remedy) is on both sides concluded, he (like the States) being the only gayner by such ciuill warres, whilst the Citizen that is the lender, is the loser: *Nam crimine ab vno disce omnes,* looke how much he snatches from one mans sheafe, hee gleanes from euery one, if they bee a hundred.

The victory being thus gotton by basenes and trechery, back comes he marching with spred colours againe to the City ; aduances in the open streete as he did before ; sels the

goods of his neighbor before his face without blushing: he
iets vp and downe in silks wouen out of other mens stocks,
feeds deliciously vpon other mens purses, rides on his ten
pound Geldings, in other mens saddles, and is now a new
man made out of wax, thats to say, out of those bonds, whose
seales he most dishonestly hath canceld. *O veluet-garded
Theeues! O yea-and-by-nay Cheaters! O ciuill, ô Graue and
Right Worshipfull Couzeners!*

What a wretchednes is it, by such steps to clime to a
counterfetted happines? So to be made for euer, is to be
vtterly vndone for euer: So for a man to saue himselfe, is to
venture his own damnation; like those that laboring by all
meanes to escape shipwrack, do afterwards desperatly drown
themselues. But alas! how rotten at the bottom are buildings
thus raised! How soone do such leases grow out of date!
The *Third House* to them is neuer heard of. What slaues
then doth mony (so purchast) make of those, who by such
wayes thinke to find out perfect freedome? But they are
most truly miserable in midst of their ioyes: for their neighbors
scorn them, Strangers poynt at them, good men neglect them,
the rich man will no more trust them, the begger in his rage
vpbraydes them. Yet if this were all, this all were nothing.
O thou that on thy pillow (lyke a Spider in his loome)
weauest mischeuous nets, beating thy braynes, how by
casting downe others, to rayse vp thy selfe!

Thou *Politick Bankrupt*, poore rich man, thou ill-painted
foole, when thou art to lye in thy last Inne (thy loathsome
graue) how heauy a loade will thy wealth bee to thy weake
corrupted Conscience! those heapes of Siluer, in telling of
which thou hast worne out thy fingers ends, will be a passing
bell, tolling in thine eare, and calling thee to a fearefull Audit.
Thou canst not dispose of thy riches, but the naming of
euery parcell will strike to thy heart, worse then the pangs
of thy departure: thy last will, at the last day, will be an
Inditement to cast thee; for thou art guilty of offending those
two lawes (enacted in the vpper House of heauen) which
directly forbid thee to steale, or to couet thy neighbors
goods.

But this is not all neither; for thou lyest on thy bed of
death, and art not carde for: thou goest out of the world, and
art not lamented: thou art put into the last linnen yat euer

thou shalt weare, (thy winding-sheete) with reproch, and
art sent into thy Graue with curses : he that makes thy
Funerall Sermon, dares not speake well of thee, because he is
asham'd to belye the dead : and vpon so hatefull a fyle doest
thou hang the records of thy life, that euen when the wormes
haue pickt thee to the bare bones, those that goe ouer thee,
will set vpon thee no Epitaph but this, *Here lyes a knaue.*

Alack ! this is not the worst neither : thy Wife being in the
heate of her youth, in the pride of her beawty, and in all the
brauery of a rich London Widow, flyes from her nest (where
she was thus fledg'd before her time) the City, to shake off
the imputation of a Bankrupts Wife, and perhaps marries
with some Gallant: thy bags then are emptied, to hold him vp
in riots: those hundreds, which thou subtilly tookst vp vpon thy
bonds, do sinfully serue him to pay Tauerne bills, and what
by knauery thou got[e]st from honest men, is as villanously
spent vpon Pandars and Whores : thy Widow being thus
brought to a low ebbe, grows desperat : curses her birth, her
life, her fortunes, yea perhaps curses thee, when thou art in
thy euerlasting sleepe, her conscience perswading strongly,
that she is punished from aboue, for thy faults : and being
poore, friendlesse, comfortlesse, she findes no meanes to raise
her selfe, but by *Falling,* and therfore growes to be a *common
woman.*   Doth not ye thought of this torment thee ?   She
liues basely by the abuse of that body, to maintaine which in
costly garments, thou didst wrong to thine owne soule : nay
more to afflict thee, thy children are ready to beg their bread
in that very place, where the father hath sat at his dore in
purple, and at his boord like *Diues,* surfeting on those dishes
which were earnd by the sweat of other mens browes.
The infortunate Marchant, whose estate is swallowed vp
by the mercilesse Seas, and the prouident Trades-man, whom
riotous Seruants at home, or hard-hearted debters abroad
vndermine and ouerthrow, blotting them with the name of
Bankrupts, deserue to be pitied and relieued, when thou that
hast cozend euen thine owne Brother of his Birth-right,
art laught at, and not remembred, but in scorne, when thou
art plagued in thy *Generation.*

Be wise therefore, you Graue, and wealthy Cittizens ; play
with these Whales of the Sea, till you escape them that are
deuourers of your Merchants ; hunt these English Wolues

to death, and rid the land of them : for these are the Rats
that eate vp the prouision of the people :· these are the
Grashoppers of *Egypt*, that spoyle the Corne-fields of the
Husbandman and the rich mans Vineyards : they will
haue poore *Naboths* piece of ground from him, though they
eate a piece of his heart for it. These are indeede (and none
but these) the *Forreners* that liue without the freedome of
your City, better than you within it ; they liue without the
freedome of honesty, of conscience, and of christianitie.
Ten dicing-houses cheate not yong Gentlemen of so much
mony in a yeare, as these do you in a moneth. The theefe that
dyes at *Tyburne* for a robbery, is not halfe so dangerous a
weede in a Common-wealth, as the *Politick Bankrupt*. I would
there were a *Derick* to hang vp him too.

The *Russians* haue an excellent custome : they beate them
on the shinnes, that haue mony, and will not pay their debts;
if that law were well cudgeld from thence into *England*,
Barbar-Surgeons might in a few yeeres build vp a Hall for their
Company, larger then Powles, only with the cure of *Bankrupt
broken-shinnes*.

I would faine see a prize set vp, that the welfed Vsurer,
and the politick Bankrupt might rayle one against another
for it : ô, it would beget a riming Comedy. The Challenge
of the *Germayne* against all the Masters of the *Noble Science*,
would not bring in a quarter of the money : for there is not
halfe so much loue betweene the Iron and the Loadestone, as
there is mortall hate betweene those two *Furies*. The Vsurer
liues by the lechery of mony, and is Bawd to his owne bags,
taking a fee, that they may ingender. The Politick Bankrupt
liues by the gelding of bags of Siluer. The Vsurer puts out
a hundred pound to breede, and let it run in a good pasture
(thats to say, in the lands that are mortgag'd for it) till it
grow great with Foale, and bring forth ten pound more. But
the Politick Bankrupt playes the Alchimist, and hauing taken
a hundred pound to multiply it, he keepes a puffing and a
blowing, as if he would fetch the Philosophers stone out of
it, yet melts your hundred pound so leng in his *Crusibles*, till
at length he either melt it cleane away, or (at the least)
makes him that lends it thinke good, if euery hundred bring
him home fiue, with Principall and Interest.

You may behold now in this *Perspectiue* piece which I haue

drawne before you, how deadly and dangerous an enemy to the State this *Politick Bankruptisme* hath bin, and still is: It hath bin long enough in the Citty, and for any thing I see, makes no great haste to get out. His triumphs haue bin great, his entertainement rich and magnificent. He purposes to lye heere as *Lucifers Legiar* : let him therefore alone in his lodging (in what part of the Citty soeuer it be) tossed and turmoyled with godlesse slumbers, and let vs take vp a standing neere some other Gate, to behold the *Entrance* of the *Second Sinne* : but before you go, looke vpon the *Chariot* that this *First* is drawne in, and take speciall note of all his Attendants.

The habit, the qualities and complexion of this Embassador sent from Hell, are set downe before. He rides in a Chariot drawne vpon three wheeles, that run fastest away, when they beare the greatest loades. The bewty of the Chariot is all in-layd work, cunningly and artificially wrought, but yet so strangely, and of so mony seuerall-fashiond pieces, (none like another) that a sound wit would mistrust they had bin stolne from sundry worke-men. By this prowd Counterfet ran two Pages ; on the left side *Conscience*, raggedly attirde, ill-fac'd, ill coloured, and misshapen in body. On the right side runs *Beggery*, who if he out-liue him, goes to serue his children. *Hipocrisy* driues the Chariot, hauing a couple of fat well-coloured and lusty Coach-horses to the eye, cald *Couetousnes* and *Cosenage*, but full of diseases, and rotten about the heart. Behind him follow a crowd of Trades-men, and Merchants, euery one of them holding either a Shopbooke, or an Obligation in his hand, their seruants, wiues and children strawing the way before him with curses, but he carelesly runnes ouer the one, and out-rides the other ; at the tayle of whom (like the *Pioners* of an Army) march troopewise, and without any Drum struck vp, because the *Leader* can abide no noyse, a company of old expert *Sarieants*, bold *Yeomen*, hungry *Baylifs*, and other braue Martiall men, who because (like the *Switzers*) they are well payd, are still in Action, and oftentimes haue the enemy in execution ; following the heeles of this Citty-Conqueror, so close, not for any loue they owe him, but only (as all those that follow great men do) to get mony by him. We will leaue them lying in Ambush, or holding their Courts of *Gard*, and take a muster of our next *Regiment*.

2. Lying.

Or,

The second dayes Triumph.

Hen it came to the eares of the *Sinfull Synagogue*, how the rich Iew of *London*, (*Barabbas Bankruptisme*) their brother, was receyued into the Citty, and what a lusty *Reueler* he was become, the rest of the same Progeny (being 6. in number) vowd to ryde thither in their greatest State, and that euery one should challenge to himselfe (if he could enter) a seuerall day of *Tryumph*; for so he might doe by their owne Customes. Another therefore of the *Broode*, being presently aptly accoustred, and armed *Cap-a-pe*, with all furniture fit for such an *Inuader*, sets forward the very next morning, and arriu'de at one of the *Gates*, before any Porters eyes were vnglewd. To knocke, hee thought it no policy, because such fellowes are commonly most churlish, when they are most intreated, and are key-cold in their comming downe to Strangers, except they be brybed: to stay there with such a confusion of faces round about him, till light should betray him, might call his Arriuall, being strange and hidden, into question; besides, he durst not send any Spy he had, to listen what newes went amongst the people, and whether any preparation were made for him, or that they did expict his approche, because indeede there was not any one of the *Damned Crewe* that followed his tayle, whom he durst trust for a true word. He resolues therefore to make his entrance, not by the sword, but by some sleyght, what storme or fayre weather soeuer should happen : And for that purpose, taking asunder his *Charriot*, (for it stood altogether like a *Germane* clock, or an English *Iack* or *Turne-spit*, vpon skrewes and vices) he scatters his Troope vpon the fielde and bye-way, into small companies, as if they had bene Irish beggers ; till at last espying certayne Colliers with Carts most sinfully loaden, for the Citty, and behind them certayne light Country Horse-women ryding to the Markets, hee mingled his Footemen carelesly amongst these, and by this *Stratagem* of Coales, brauely thorow *Moore-gate*, got within the walles, where marching not like a plodding *Grasyer* with his *Droues* before him, but like a *Citty-Captayne*, with a Company (as pert as Taylours at a wedding) close at his heeles, (because nowe they knewe they were out of feare) hee musters together all the *Hackneymen* and *Horse-coursers* in and about *Colman-streete*.

No sooner had these Sonnes and Heyres vnto Horse-shooes, got him into their eyes, but they wept for ioy to behold him ; yet in the ende, putting vp their teares into bottles of Hay, which they held vnder their armes, and wyping their slubberd cheekes with wispes of cleane Strawe (prouyed for the nonce) they harnessed the *Grand Signiors* Caroach, mounted his *Cauallery* vpon Curtals, and so sent him most pompously (like a new elected *Dutch Burgomaster*) into the Citty.

He was lookt vpon strangely by all whom he met, for at the first, few or none knew him, few followed him, few bid him welcome : But after hee had spent heere a very little peece of time, after it was voyc'd that *Monsieur Mendax* came to dwell amongst them, and had brought with him all sorts of politick falshood and lying, what a number of Men, Women and Children fell presently in loue with him ! There was of euery Trade in the City, and of euery profession some, that instantly were dealers with him : For you must note, that in a State so multitudinous, where so many flocks of people must be fed, it is impossible to haue some Trades to stand, if they should not *Lye*.

How quickly after the Art of *Lying* was once publiquely profest, were false *Weights* and false *Measures* inuented ! and they haue since done as much hurt to the inhabitants of Citties, as the inuention of *Gunnes* hath done to their walles : for though a *Lye* haue but short legs (like a Dwarfes) yet

it goes farrè in a little time, *Et crescit eundo,* and at last
prooues a tall fellow : the reason is, that *Truth* had euer but
one *Father,* but *Lyes* are a thousand mens *Bastards,* and are
begotten euery where.

Looke vp then (*Thou thy Countryes Darling,*) and behold
what a diuelish *Inmate* thou hast intertained. The *Genealogy*
of *Truth* is well knowne, for she was borne in Heauen,
and dwels in Heauen: *Falshood* then and *Lying* must of
necessity come out of that hot Country of Hell, from the
line of Diuels: for those two are as opposite, as day and
darkenes. What an vngracious *Generation* wilt thou mingle
with thine, if thou draw not *this* from thee : What a number
of vnhappy and cursed children will be left vpon thy hand ?
for *Lying* is Father to *Falshood,* and Grandsire to *Periury* :
Frawd (with two faces) is his Daughter, a very Monster :
Treason (with haires like Snakes) is his kinsemen ; a very
Fury! how art thou inclos'd with danger ? The *Lye* first
deceiues thee, and to shoote the deceit off cleanly, an oath
(like an Arrow) is drawne to the head, and that hits the
marke. If a *Lye,* after it is mo[u]lded, be not smooth enough,
there is no instrument to burnish it, but an oath : Swearing
giues it cullor, and a bright complexion. So that *Oathes* are
Crutches, vpon whych *Lyes* (like lame soldiers) go, and neede
no other pasport. Little oathes are able to beare vp great
lyes : but great *Lyes* are able to beate downe great *Families* :
For oathes are wounds that a man stabs into himselfe, yea,
they are burning words that consume those who kindle them.

What fooles then are thy *Buyers* and *Sellers* to be abused
by such hell-hounds ? *Swearing* and *Forswearing* put into
their hands perhaps the gaines of a little Siluer, but like
those pieces which *Iudas* receiued, they are their destruction.
Welth so gotten, is like a tree set in the depth of winter, it
prospers not.

But is it possible (*Thou leader of so great a Kingdome*) that
heretofore so many bonfires of mens bodies should be made
before thee in the good quarrell of *Trueth* ? and that now
thou shouldst take part with her enemy ? Haue so many
Triple-pointed darts of *Treason* bin shot at the heads of thy
Princes, because they would not take *Truth* out of thy *Temples,*
and art thou now in *League* with false *Witches* yat
would kill thee ? Thou art no Traueler, the habit of Lying
therefore will not become thee, cast it off.

3 *

He that giues a soldier the *Lye*, lookes to receiue the stab : but what danger does he run vpon, that giues a whole City the *Lye* ? yet must I venture to giue it thee.   Let me tell thee then, that *Thou doest Lye* with *Pride*, and though thou art not so gawdy, yet art thou more costly in attiring thy selfe than the Court, because *Pride* is the *Queene of Sinnes*, thou hast chosen her to be thy *Concubine*, and hast begotten many base Sonnes and Daughters vpon her body, as *Vainglory, Curiosity, Disobedience, Opinion, Disdaine*, &c. *Pride*, by thy *Lying* with her, is growne impudent : She is now a common Harlot, and euery one hath vse of her body.   The *Taylor* calls her his *Lemman*, he hath often got her great with child of *Phantasticallity* and *Fashions*, who no sooner came into the world, but the fairest Wiues of thy Tennants snatcht them vp into their armes, layd them in their laps and to their brests, and after they had plaid with them their pleasure, into the country were those two children (of the *Taylors*) sent to be nurst vp, so that they liue sometimes there, but euer and anon with thee.

Thou doest likewise *Lye* with *Vsury* : how often hast thou bin found in bed with her !   How often hath she bin openly disgraced at the Crosse for a Strumpet ! yet still doest thou keepe her company, and art not ashamed of it, because you commit Sinne together, euen in those houses that haue paynted posts standing at the Gates.   What vngodly brats and kindred hath she brought thee ? for vpon *Vsury* hast thou begotten *Extortion*, (a strong, but an vnmannerly child,) *Hardnes of heart*, a very murderer, and *Bad Conscience*, who is so vnruly, that he seemes to be sent vnto thee, to be thy euerlasting paine.   Then hath she Sonnes in law, and they are all *Scriueners* : those *Scriueners* haue base sonnes, and they are all common *Brokers* ; those *Brokers* likewise send a number into the world, and they are all *Common Theeues*.

All of these may easily giue Armes : for they fetch their discent from hell, where are as many Gentlemen, as in any one place, in any kingdome.

Thou doost lye with sundrie others, and committest strange whoredomes, which by vse and boldnesse growe so common, that they seeme to be no whoredomes at all, Yet thine owne abhominations would not appeare so vilely, but that thou makest thy buildings a *Brothelry* to others : for thou

sufferest *Religion* to lye with *Hipocrisie* : *Charity* to lye with
Ostentation : *Friendship* to lye with *Hollow - heartednes* : the
Churle to lye with *Simony* : *Iustice* to lye with *Bribery* : and
last of all, *Conscience* to lye with euerie one, So that now shee
is full of diseases : But thou knowest the medicine for al these
Feauers that shake thee : be therfore to thy selfe thine owne
Phisitian, and by strong Pilles purge away this second
infection that is breeding vpon thee, before it strike to the
heart.

Falshood and *Lying* thus haue had their day, and like
Almanackes of the last yeare, are now gon out : let vs follow
them a step or two farther to see how they ride, and then
(if we can) leaue them, for I perceiue it growes late, because
Candle-light (who is next to enter vpon the stage) is making
himself ready to act his Comicall Scenes. The *Chariot* then
that *Lying* is drawne in, is made al of whetstones ; Wantonnes
and euil custome are his Horses ; a Foole is the Coachman that
driues them : a couple of swearing *Fencers* sometimes leade
the Horses by the reynes, and sometimes flourish before them
to make roome. Worshipfully is this Lord of *Limbo* attended,
for Knights themselues follow close at his heeles ; Mary they
are not *Post* and *Poyre* - Knightes but one of the *Post*.
Amongst whose traine is shuffled in a company of scambling
ignorant *Petti-foggars*, leane Knaues and hungrie, for they
liue vpon nothing but the scraps of the Law, and heere and
there (like a Prune in White-broth) is stucke a spruice, but a
meere prating vnpractised Lawyers Clarke all in blacke. At
the tayle of all (when this goodly Pageant is passed by) follow
a crowde of euerie trade some, amongst whome least we be
smothered, and bee taken to bee of the same list, let vs strike
downe my way.

Namque odi profanum Vulgus.

3. Candle-light.

Or,

The Nocturnall Tryumph.

Candle-light! and art thou one of the *Cursed Crew*? hast thou bin set at the Table of Princes, and Nobelmen? haue all sortes of people doone reuerence vnto thee, and stood bare so soone as euer they haue seene thee? haue *Theeues, Traytors,* and *Murderers* been affraide to come in thy presence, because they knewe thee iust, and that thou wouldest discouer them? And art thou now a harborer of all kindes of *Vices*? nay, doost thou play the capitall *Vice* thy selfe?

Hast thou had so many learned *Lectures* read before thee, and is the light of thy *Vnderstanding* now cleane put out, and haue so many profound schollers profited by thee? hast thou doone such good to *Vniuersities,* beene soch a guide to the Lame, and seene the dooing of so many good workes, yet doest thou now looke dimly, and with a dull eye vpon al *Goodnes*? What comfort haue sickmen taken (in weary and irkesome nights) but onely in thee? thou hast been their Phisition and Apothecary, and when the rellish of nothing could please them, the very shadow of thee hath beene to them a restoratiue *Consolation.* The Nurse hath stilled her wayward Infant, shewing it but to thee. What gladnes hast thou put into *Mariners* bosomes, when thou hast met them on the Sea? What Ioy into the faint and benighted *Trauailer* when he has met thee on the land? How many poore *Handy-craftes* men by *Thee* haue earned the best part of their liuing? And art thou now become a *Companion* for Drunkards, for leachers, and for prodigalles? Art thou turnd *Reprobate*? thou wilt burne for it in hell, And so odious is this thy *Apostacy*, and hiding thy self from ye light of the truth, yat thy death and going out of the world, euen they yat loue thee best, wil tread thee vnder their feete : yea I yat haue thus plaid the Herrald, and proclaimed thy good parts, wil now play the Cryer and cal thee into open count, to arraigne thee for thy misdemeanors.

Let the world therefore vnderstand, that this Tallow-facde Gentleman (cald *Candle-light*) so soone as euer the Sunne was gon[e] out of sight, and that darkenes like a thief out of a hedge crept vpon the earth, sweate till hee dropt agen, with bustling to come into the *Cittie*. For hauing no more but one onely eye (and that fierie red with drinking and sitting vp late) he was ashamed to be seene by day, knowing he should be laught to scorne, and hooted at. He makes his entrance therefore at *Aldersgate* of set purpose, for though the streete be faire and spatious, yet few lightes in mistie euenings, vsing there to thrust out their golden heads he thought that the aptest circle for him to be raised in, because there his *Glittering* would make greatest show.

What expectation was there of his comming? setting aside ye bonfiers, there is not more triumphing on Midsommer night. No sooner was he aduaunced vp into the moste famous Streetes, but a number of shops for ioy beganne to shut in : Mercers rolde vp their silkes and Veluets : the Goldsmithes drew backe their Plate, and all the City lookt like a priuate Play-house, when the windowes are clapt downe, as if some *Nocturnal*, or dismall *Tragedy* were presently to be acted before all the *Trades-men*. But *Caualiero Candle-light* came for no such solemnitie : No he had other Crackers in hand to which hee wacht but his houre to giue fire. Scarce was his entrance blown abroad, but the Bankrupt, the Fellon, and all that owed any mony, and for feare of arrests, or Iustices warrants, had like so many Snayles kept their houses ouer their heads al the day before, began now to creep out of their shels, and to stalke vp and down the streets as vprightly, and with as proud a gate as if they meant to knock against the starres with the crownes of their heads.

The damask-coated Cittizen, that sat in his shop both

forenoone and afternoone, and lookt more sowerly on his poore neighbors, then if he had drunke a quart of Vineger at a draught, sneakes out of his owne doores, and slips into a Tauerne, where either alone, or with some other that battles their money together, they so plye themselues with penny pots, which (like small-shot) goe off, powring into their fat paunches, that at length they haue not an eye to see withall, nor a good legge to stand vpon. In which pickle if anye of them happen to be iustled downe by a post (that in spite of them will take the wall) and so reeles them into the kennell, who takes them vp or leades them home? who has them to bed, and with a pillow smothes this stealing so of good liquor, but that brazen-face *Candle-light*? Nay more, hee intices their verie Prentices to make their desperate sallyes out, and quicke retyres in (contrarie to the Oath of their Indentures) which are seuen yeares a swearing, onely for their Pintes, and away.

Tush, this is nothing! yong shopkeepers that haue newly ventured vpon the pikes of marriage, who are euery houre shewing their wares to their Customers, plying their businesse harder all day then *Vulcan* does his Anuile, and seeme better husbands than *Fidlers* that scrape for a poore liuing both day and night, yet euen these if they can but get *Candle-light*, to sit vp all night with them in any house of *Reckning* (thats to say in a *Tauerne*) they fall roundly to play the *London* prize, and thats at three seuerall weapons, *Drinking*, *Dauncing*, and *Dicing*, Their wiues lying all that time in their beds sighing like widowes, which is lamentable: the giddie-braind husbands wasting the portions they had with them, which lost once, they are (like Maiden-heades) neuer recouerable. Or which is worse, this going a Bat-fowling a nights, beeing noted by some wise yong-man or other, that knowes how to handle such cases, the bush is beaten for them at home, whilest they catch the bird abroade, but what bird is it? the Woodcocke.

Neuer did any Cittie pocket vp such wrong at the hands of one, ouer whom she is so iealous, and so tender, that in Winter nights if he be but missing, and hide himselfe in the darke, I know not how many Beadles are sent vp and downe the streetes to crie him: yet you see, there is more cause she should send out to curse him. For what Villanies are not

abroad so long as *Candle-light* is stirring? The *Seruing-man*
dare then walke with his wench: the *Priuate Puncke* (otherwise
called one that boords in *London*) who like a Pigeon sits
billing all day within doores, and feares to steppe ouer the
thresholde, does then walke the round till midnight, after she
hath beene swaggering amongst pottle pots and Vintners
boyes. Nay, the sober *Perpetuana* suited Puritane, that
dares not (so much as by Moone-light) come neere the
Suburb-shadow of a house, where they set stewed Prunes
befor[e] you, raps as boldly at the hatch, when he knowes
Candle-light is within, as if he were a new chosen Constable.
When al doores are lockt vp, when no eyes are open, when
birds sit silent in bushes, and beasts lie sleeping vnder
hedges, when no creature can be smelt to be vp but they that
may be smelt euery night a streets length ere you come at
them, euen then doth this *Ignis fatuus* (*Candle-light*) walke
like a· Fire-drake into sundrie corners. If you will not
beleeue this, shoote but your eye through the Iron grates
into the Cellers of Vintners, there you shall see him hold
his necke in a Iin, made of a clift hoope-sticke, to throttle
him from telling tales, whilest they most abhominably iumble
together all the papisticall drinkes that are brought from
beyond-sea : the poore wines are rackt and made to confesse
anie thing : the Spanish and the French meeting both in the
bottome of the Cellar, conspire together in their cups, to lay
the *Englishman* (if he euer come into their company) vnder
the boord.

To be short, such strange mad musick doe they play vpon
their Sacke-buttes, that if *Candle-light* beeing ouer come with
the steeme of newe sweete Wines, when they are at worke,
shoulde not tell them tis time to goe to bedde, they would
make all the Hogges-heads that vse to come to the house,
to daunce the Cannaries till they reeld againe. When the
Grape-mongers and hee are parted, hee walkes vp and downe
the streetes squiring olde Midwiues to anie house, (verie
secretly) where any Bastards are to be brought into the worlde.
From them, (about the houre when Spirits walke, and Cats
goe a gossipping) hee visits the Watch, where creeping into
the *Beadles* Cothouse (which standes betweene his legges,
that are lapt rounde about with peeces of Rugge, as if he
had newe strucke of[f] Shackles) and seeing the Watch-men

to nodde at him, hee hydes himselfe presently, (knowing the token) vnder the flappe of a gowne, and teaches them (by instinct) howe to steale nappes into their heades, because hee sees all their Cloakes haue not one good nappe vppon them: and vppon his warrant snort they so lowde, that to those Night walkers (whose wittes are vp so late) it serues as a Watch-worde to keepe out of the reach of their browne Billes: by which meanes they neuer come to aunswere the matter before maister Constable, and the Bench vppon which his men (that shoulde watch) doe sitte: so that the Counters are cheated of Prisoners, to the great dammage of those that shoulde haue their mornings draught out of the Garnish.

O *Candle-light, Candle-light*! to howe manie costly Sacke-possets, and reare Banquets hast thou beene inuited by Prentices and Kitchen-maidens?   When the *Bell-man* for anger to spie (such a Purloyner of Cittizens goods) so many, hath bounced at the doore like a madde man, At which (as if *Robin Good-fellow* had beene coniur'd vp amongst them) the Wenches haue falne into the handes of the Greene-sicknesse, and the yong fellowes into colde Agues, with verie feare least their maister (like olde *Ieronimo* and *Isabella* his wife after him) starting out of his naked bed should come downe (with a Weapon in his hande) and this in his mouth: *What out-cryes pull vs from our naked bedde? Who calles?* &c. as the Players can tell you. O *Candle-light*, howe hast thou stuncke then, when they haue popt thee out of their companye; howe hast thou taken it in snuffe, when thou hast beene smelt out especially the maister of the house exclayming, that by day that deede of darknesse had not beene.   One Vennie more with thee, and then I haue done.

How many lips haue beene worne out with kissing at the street doore, or in ye entry (in a winking blind euening?) how many odde matches and vneuen mariages haue been made there betweene young Prentises and there maisters daughters, whilest thou (O *Candle-light*) hast stood watching at the staires heade, that none could come stealing downe by thee, but they must bee seene?

It appeares by these articles put in against thee, that thou art partly a Bawd to diuerse loose sinnes, and partly a Coozener: for if any in the Cittie haue badde wares lying deade vppon their handes, thou art better than *Aqua vitæ* to fetch life into them, and to sende them packing. Thou shalt therefore bee taken out of thy proude Chariot, and bee carted: yet first will wee see what workmanship, and what stuffe it is made of, to the intent that if it bee not daungerous for a Cittie to keepe anie Relique belonging to such a crooked Saint, It .may bee hung vp as a monument to shewe with what dishonour thou wert driuen out of so noble a lodging, to deface whose buildings thou hast beene so enuious, that when thou hast beene left alone by any thing that woulde take fire, thou hast burnt to the ground many of her goodlyest houses.

Candle lights Coach is made all of Horne, shauen as thin as Changelinges are. It is drawne (with ease) by two *Rats*: the *Coachman* is a *Chaundler*, who so sweats with yeacking them, that he drops tallowe, and that feedes them as prouender: yet are the lashes that hee giues the squeaking *Vermine* more deadly to them then al the the *Ratsbane* in Bucklersburie. *Painefulnesse* and *Studdy* are his two Lackeyes and run by him: *Darkuesse, Conspiracy, Opportunitie, Stratagems* and *Feare*, are his attendants : hee's sued vnto by *Diggars* in *Mines, Grauers, Schollers, Mariners, Nurses, Drunkards, Vnthriftes* and shrode *Husbands*: hee destroyes that which feedes him, and therefore *Ingratitude* comes behinde all this, driuing them before her. The next Diuel that is to be commaunded vp, is a very lazie one, and will be long in rising : let vs therefore vnbinde this, and fall to other Charmes.

4. Sloth

Or

The fourth dayes Tryumph.

An (doubtlesse) was not created to bee an idle fellow, for then he should bee Gods *Vagabond*: he was made for other purpose then to be euer eating as swine : euer sleeping as *Dormise* : euer dumb as fishes in the Sea, or euer prating to no purpose, as birdes of the ayre : he was not set in this *Vniuersall Orchard* to stand still as a *Tree,* and so to bee cut downe, but to be cut downe if he should stand still. And to haue him remember this, he carries certaine *Watches* with *Larums* about him, that are euer striking : for all the *Enginous Wheeles* of the *Soule* are continually going : though the body lye neuer so fast bownde in Slumbers, the imagination runnes too and fro, the phantasie flyes round about, the vitall Spirits walke vp and downe, yea the very pulses shew actiuitie, and with their hammers are still beating, so that euen in his very dreames it is whispered in his eare that hee must bee dooing something.

If hee had not these prompters at his elbowe yet euerie member of his body (if it could speake would chide him) if they were put to no vse, considering what noble workmanship is bestowed vpon them. For man no sooner gets vpon his legges, but they are made so that either hee may run or goe : when he is weary, they can giue him ease by standing still, if he will not stand, the *Knees* serue like Hindges to bow

vp and downe, and to let him kneele. His armes haue
artificiall cordes and stringes, which shorten or flye out of
their length at pleasure : They winde about the bodye like
a siluer Girdle, and being held out before, are weapons to
defend it : at the end of the armes are two beautiful
Mathematicall Instruments, with fiue seuerall motions in
each of them, and thirtie other mouing *Engines*, by which
they stirre both. His head likewise standes vppon three
Skrewes, the one is directly forward to teach him *Prouidence*,
the other two are on eather side one, to arme him with
Circumspection : How busie are both the eyes, to keepe
danger from him euerie way.

But admit hee had none of these *Wonderfull Volumes* to
reade ouer, yet hee sees the clowdes alwaies working : the
waters euer labouring : the earth continuallye bringing foorth :
he sees the Sunne haue a hye colour with taking paines for
the day. The Moone pale and sickly, with sitting vp for the
night : the Stars mustring their armyes together to guard
the Moone. All of them, and all that is in the world, seruing
as Schoolemaisters, and the world it selfe as an *Academ*[*y*] to
bring vp man in knowledge, and to put him still into action.

How then dares this nastie, and loathsome sin of *Sloth*
venture into a Citie amongst so many people ? who doth he
hope wil giue him entertainment ? what lodging (thinks he)
can be taine vp, where he and his heauy-headed company
may take their afternoones nap soundly? for in euery street,
carts and Coaches make such a thundring as if the world
ranne vpon wheeles : at euerie corner, men, women, and
children meete in such shoales, that postes are sette vp of
purpose to strengthen the houses, least with iustling one
another they should shoulder them downe. Besides, hammers
are beating in one place, Tubs hooping in another, Pots
clincking in a third, water-tankards running at tilt in a
fourth : heere are Porters sweating vnder burdens, there
Marchants-men bearing bags of money, Chapmen (as if they
were at Leape frog) skippe out of one shop into another :
Tradesmen (as if they were dauncing Galliards) are lusty at
legges and neuer stand still : all are as busie as countrie
Atturneyes at an Assises : how then can *Idlenes* thinke to
inhabit heere ?

Yet the *Worshipfull Sir*, (that leades a Gentlemans life,

and dooth nothing) though he comes but slowly on (as if hee trodde a French March) yet hee comes and with a great trayne at his tayle, as if the countrie had brought vp some *Fellon* to one of our Gayles, So is he conuaide by nine or tenne drowsie Malt-men, that lye nodding ouer their Sackes, and euen a moste sleepie and still Triumph begins his entrance at *Bishopsgate.*

An armie of substantiall Housholders (moste of them liuing by the hardnesse of the hand) came in Battaile array, with spred Banners, bearing the Armes of their seuerall occupations to meete this *Cowardly Generall* and to beate him backe. But hee sommoning a parlee, hammered out such a strong Oration in praise of *Ease,* that they all strucke vp their Drums, flung vp their *Round-Cappes,* (and as if it had beene another *William* the *Conqueror* came marching in with him) and lodged him in the quietest streete in the Cittie, for so his *Lazinesse* requested.

Hee then presently gaue licenses to all the Vintners, to keepe open house, and to emptye their Hogsheades to all commers, who did so, dying their grates into a drunkards blush (to make them knowe from Grates of a prison) least customers should reele away from them and hanging out new bushes, that if men at their going out, could not see the signe, yet they might not loose themselues in the bush. He likewise gaue order that dicing-houses, and bowling alleyes should be erected, wherupon a number of poore handy-crafts-men, that before wrought night and day, made stocks to themselues of ten groates, and crowns a peece, and what by Betting, Lurches, Rubbers and such tricks, they neuer tooke care for a good daies worke afterwards. For as *Letchery* is patron of al your Suburb Colledges, and sets vp *Vaulting-houses,* and *Daunsing-Schooles* : and as *Drunkennesse* when it least can stand, does best hold vp Alehouses, So *Sloth* is a founder of the Almeshouses first mentioned, and is a good Benefactor to these last.

The Players prayed for his comming, they lost nothing by it, the comming in of tenne Embassadors was neuer so sweete to them, as this our sinne was; their houses smoakt euerye after noone with Stinkards, who were so glewed together in crowdes with the Steames of strong breath, that when they came foorth, their faces lookt as if they had

beene perboylde : And his *Comicall Tearme-time* they hoped
for, at the least all the summer, because tis giuen out that
Sloth himselfe will come, and sit in the two-pennie galleries
amongst the Gentlemen, and see their *Knaueries* and their
pastimes.

But alas ! if these were the sorest diseases (*Thou noblest
City of the now-noblest Nation*) that *Idlenesse* does infect thee
with : thou hast Phisick sufficient in thy selfe, to purge thy
bodie of them. No, no, hee is not slothfull, that is onelye
lazie, that onelye waistes his good houres, and his Siluer in
Luxury, and licentious ease, or that onely (like a standing
water) does nothing, but gather corruption : no, hee is the
true *Slothfull* man that does no good. And how many would
crie *Guilty* vnto thee, if this were there *Inditement*? Thy
Maiestrates (that when they see thee most in danger) put
vp the swordes that *Iustice* hath guided, to their loynes, and
flie into the countrie, leauing thee destitute of their *Counsell*,
they would crie guilty, they are slothfull.

Thy Phisitions, that fearing to die by that which they
liue, (*sicknes*) doe most vnkindely leaue thee when thou art
ready to lye, vpon thy death bed, *They* are slothful, *They*
would crie Guilty. Thy great men, and such as haue been
thy *Rulers*, that being taken out of poore Cradles, and nursed
vp by thee, haue fild their Cofers with golde, and their
names with honour, yet afterwards growing weary of thee,
(like *Mules* hauing suckt their dammes) most ingratefully
haue they stolne from thee, spending those blessings which
were thine, vpon those that no way deserue them. Are not
These Slothfull? They would crie guiltye. There is yet one
more, whome I would not heare to *Cry Guilty*, because (of
all others) I would not haue them slothfull. O you that
speake the language of *Angels*, and should indeed be *Angels*
amongst vs, you that haue offices aboue those of Kinges,
that haue warrant to commaund Princes, and controle them,
if they do amisse : you that are Stewards ouer the Kings
house of heauen, and lye heere as Embassadors about the
greatest State-matters in the world : what a dishonour were
it to your places, if it should bee knowne that you are
Sloathfull ? you are sworne labourers, to worke in a Vineyard,
which if you dresse not carefully, if you cut it not artificially,
if you vnderprop it not wisely when you see it laden, if you

gather not the fruites in it, when they bee ripe, but suffer them to drope downe, and bee eaten vp by Swine. O what a deere account are you to make him that must giue you your hire ? you are the Beames of the Sun that must ripen the grapes of the Vine, and if you shine not cleerely, he will eclipse you for euer : your tongues are the instruments that must cut off rancke and idle Sprigs, to make the bearing-braunches to spred, and vnlesse you keep them sharpe and be euer pruning with them, he will cast you by, and you shall be eaten vp with rust. The Church is a garden and you must weede it : it is a Fountaine, and you must keepe it cleere : it is her Husbands Jewell, and you must pollish it : it is his best belooued, and you must keepe her chast.

Many Merchants hath this Cittie to her Sonnes, of al which you are the most noble, you trafficke onely for mens Soules, sending them to the Land of *Promise*, and to the heauenly *Ierusalem*, and receiuing from thence (in *Exchange*) the richest Commoditie in the world, your owne saluation. O therefore bee not you Slothfull : for if being chosen Pilots, you Sleepe, and so sticke vpon Rockes, you hazard your owne shipwracke more then theirs that venture with you.

What a number of Colours are heere grounded, to paint out *Sloth* in his vglines, and to make him loathed, whilst he (yawning, and his Chin knocking nods into his brest) regardes not the whips of the moste crabbish *Satyristes*. Let vs therfore looke vpon his *Horse-litter* that hee rides in, and so leaue him.

A couple of vnshodde Asses carry it betweene them, it is all fluttishly ouergrowne with Mosse on the out-side, and on the inside quilted through out with downe pillowes : *Sleepe* and *Plenty* leade the *Fore-Asse* ; a pursie double chind *Læna*, riding by on a Sumpter-horse with prouander at his mouth, and she is the *Litter-Driuer* : shee keepes two Pages, and those are an *Irish Beggar* one the one side, and *One that sayes he has been a Soldier* on the other side. His attendants are *Sicknes, Want, Ignorance, Infamy, Bondage, Palenes, Blockishnes,* and *Carelesnes.* The Retayners that wear his cloth are *Anglers, Dumb Ministers, Players, Exchange-Wenches, Gamsters, Panders, Whores* and *Fidlers.*

Apishnesse:
Or
The fift dayes Triumph

Loth was not so slow in his march, when hee entred the Citie, but *Apishnesse* (that was to take his turne next) was as quick. Do you not know him? It cannot be read in any Chronicle, that he was euer with *Henrie* the eight at *Bulloigne* or at ye winning of *Turwin* and *Turnay*: for (not to belie the *sweete Gentleman*,) he was neither in the shell then, no nor then when *Paules-steeple* and the Weathercocke were on fire; by which markes (without looking in his mouth) you may safely sweare, that hees but yong, for hees a feirse, dapper fellow, more light headed then a Musitian: as phantastically attyred as a Court Ieaster: wanton in discourse: lasciuious in behauiour; iocond in good companie: nice in his trencher, and yet he feedes verie hungerly on scraps of songs: he drinkes in a Glasse well, but vilely in a deepe French-bowle: yet much about the yeare when *Monsieur* came in, was hee begotten, betweene a French Tayler, and an English Court-Seamster. This *Signior Ioculento* (as the diuell would haue it) comes prawncing in at *Cripplegate*, and he may well doe it, for indeede all the parts hee playes are but con'd speeches stolne from others, whose voices and actions he counterfeites: but so lamely, that all the Cripples in tenne Spittle-houses, shewe not more halting. The *Grauer Browes* were bent against him, and by the awfull *Charms* of *Reuerend Authoritie*, would haue sent him

downe frome whence he came, for they knew howe smooth
soeuer his lookes were, there was a diuell in his bosome :
But hee hauing the stronger faction on his side, set them in
a Mutenie, *Sæuitque animis ignobile vulgus*, the manie headed
Monster fought as it had beene against Saint *George*, won
the gate, and then with showtes was the *Gaueston of the
Time*, brought in. But who brought him in ? None but
richmens sonnes that were left well, and had more money
giuen by will, then they had wit how to bestow it : none but
Prentises almost out of their yeers, and all the Tailors,
Haberdashers, and Embroderers that could be got for loue
or money, for these were prest secretly to the seruice, by the
yong and wanton dames of the Citie, because they would not
be seene to shewe their loue to him themselues.

Man is Gods Ape, and an Ape is *Zani* to a man, doing ouer
those trickes (especially if they be knauish) which hee sees
done before him : so that *Apishnesse* is nothing but counter-
fetting or imitation : and this flower when it first came into
the Citie, had a prettie scent, and a delightfull colour, hath
bene let to run so high, that it is now seeded, and where it
fals there rises vp a stinking weede.

For as man is Gods ape, striuing to make artificiall
flowers, birdes, &c. like to the natural : So for the same
reason are women, Mens *Shee Apes*, for they will not bee behind
them the bredth of a Taylors yard (which is nothing to
speake of) in anie new-fangled vpstart fashion. If men get
vp French standing collers, women will haue the French
standing coller too : if Dublets with little thick skirts, (so
short that none are able to sit vpon them), womens foreparts
are thick skirted too : by surfetting vpon which kinde of
phantasticall *Apishnesse* in a short time, they fall into the
disease of pride : Pride is infectious, and breedes prodigalitie :
Prodigalitie after it has runne a little, closes vp and festers,
and then turnes to *Beggerie*. Wittie was that Painter therefore,
that when hee had limned one of euery Nation in their
proper attyres, and beeing at his wittes endes howe to drawe
an *Englishman*, At the last (to giue him a quippe for his
follie in apparell) drewe him starke naked, with Sheeres in
his hand, and cloth on his arme, because none could cut
out his fashions but himselfe.

For an English-mans suite is like a traitors bodie that

hath beene hanged, drawne, and quartered, and is set vp in
seuerall places: his Codpeece is in *Denmarke*, the collor of
his Duble[t], and the belly in *France*: the wing and narrowe
sleeue in *Italy*; the short waste hangs ouer a *Dutch* Botchers
stall in *Vtrich*: his huge floppes speakes *Spanish*: *Polonia*
giues him the Boates: the blocke for his heade alters faster then
the Feltmaker can fitte him, and thereupon we are called in
scorne *Blockheades*. And thus we that mocke euerie Nation,
for keeping one fashion, yet steale patches from euerie one
of them, to peece out our pride, are now laughing-stocks to
them, because their cut so scuruily becomes vs:

This sinne of *Apishnesse*, whether it bee in apparell, or in
diet, is not of such long life as his fellowes, and for seeing none
but women and fooles keepe him companie, the one will be
ashamed of him when they begin to haue wrinckles, the other
when they feele their purses light. The Magistrate, the
wealthy commoner, and the auncient Cittizen, disdaine to
come neare him: wee were best therefore, take note of such
things as are aboute him, least on a suddaine hee slip out of
sight.

Apishnesse rides in a Chariot made of nothing but cages, in
which are all the strangest out-landish Birds that can be
gotten: the Cages are stucke full of Parats feathers: the
Coach-man is an *Italian Mownti-banck* who driues a Fawne
and a Lambe, for they drawe the Gew-gaw in Winter, when
such beasts are rarest to be had: In Sommer, it goes alone
by the motion of wheeles: two Pages in light coloured suites,
embrodered full of Butterflies, with wings that flutter vp
with the winde, run by him, the one being a dauncing boy
the other a Tumbler: His attendants are *Folly, Laughter,
Inconstancie, Riot, Nicenesse,* and *Vainglorie*: when his Court
remoues, hee is folowed by *Tobacconists, Shittlecock-makers,
Feathermakers, Cob-web-lawne-weauers, Perfumers,* young,
Countrie *Gentlemen,* and *Fooles,* In whose Ship whilest they
all are sayling, let vs obserue what other abuses the
Verdimotes Inquest doe present on the lande, albeit they bee
neuer reformed, till a second *Chaos* is to bee refined. In the
meane time, *In noua fert Animus.*

4 *

Shauing:

Or

The sixt dayes Triumph.

Ow ? *Shauing*! Me thinkes *Barbers* should crie to their Customers winck hard and come running out of their shoppes into the open streetes, throwing all their Suddes out of their learned Latin Basons into my face for presuming to name the *Mysterie* of *Shauing* in so villanous a companie as these seuen are. Is that Trade (say they) that for so many yeares hath beene held vp by so many heades, and has out-bearded the stowtest in *England* to their faces, Is that *Trade*, that because it is euermore *Trimming* the Citie, hath beene for many yeers past made vp into a Societie, and hath their *Guild*, and their *Priuiledges* with as much freedome as the best, must that nowe bee counted a sinne (nay and one of the *Deadly sinnes*) of the Cittie? No, no, be not angry with me, (O you that bandie away none but sweete washing Balles, and cast none other then Rose-waters for any mans pleasure) for there is *Shauing* within the *walles* of this *Great Metropolis*, which you neuer dreamed of: A shauing that takes not only away the rebellious haires, but brings the flesh with it too: and if that cannot suffice, the very bones must follow. If therfore you, and *Fiue* companies greater then yours, should chuse a Colonel, to lead you against this mightie *Tamburlaine*, you are too weake to make him *Retire*, and if you should come to a batteil, you would loose the day.

· For behold what *Troopes* forsake the *Standard* of the Citie, and flie to him : neither are they base and common souldiers, but euen those that haue borne armes a long time. Be silent therfore, and be patient : and since there is no remedie but that (*this combatant that is so cunning at the sharp*) wil come in, mark in what triumphant and proud manner, he is marshalled through *Newgate* : At which *Bulwarke* (and none other) did he (in policy) desire to shew himself. First, because he knew if the Citie should play with him as they did with *Wiat*, *Newgate* held a number, that though they were false to all the world, would be true to him. Couragiously therfore does he enter : All of them that had once serued vnder his colors (and were now to suffer for the *Truth*, which they had abused) leaping vp to the Iron lattaces, to beholde their *General*, and making such a ratling with shaking their chaines for ioy, as if *Cerberus* had bin come from hell to liue and die amongst them. *Shauing* is now lodged in the heart of the Citie, but by whom ? and at whose charges ? Mary at a common purse, to which many are tributaries, and therfore no maruell if he be feasted royally. The first that paid their mony towards it, are cruel and couetous Land-lords, who for the building vp of a Chimny, which stands them not aboue 30.s. and for whiting the wals of a tenement, which is scarce worth the daubing raise the rent presently (as if it were new put into ye Subsidy book) assessing it at 3. li. a yeer more then euer it went for before : filthy wide-mouthd bandogs they are, that for a quarters rent will pull out their ministers throte, if he were their tenant : And (though it turn to the vtter vndoing of a man) being rubd with quicksiluer, which they loue because they haue mangy consciences, they will let to a drunken *Flemming* a house ouer his own country-man head, thinking hees safe enough from the thunderbolts of their wiues and children, and from curses, and the very vengeance of heauen, if he get by the bargaine, but so many Angels as will couer the crowne of his head.

The next that laide downe his share, was no Sharer among the Players, but a shauer of yong *Gentlemen*, before euer a haire dare peepe out of their chinnes : and these are *Vsurers* : who for a little money, and a greate deal of trash : (as Fire-shouels, browne-paper, motley cloake-bags, &c.) bring yong Nouices into a fooles Paradice till they haue sealed the

Morgage of their landes, and then like Pedlers, goe they (or
some Familiar spirit for them raizde by the *Vsurers*) vp and
downe to cry *Commodities*, which scarce yeeld the third part
of ye sum for which they take them vp.

There are likewise other Barbers,who are so well customed,
that they shaue a whole Citie sometymes in three dayes, and
they doe it (as *Bankes* his horse did his *tricks*) onely by the eye,
and the eare : For if they either see no Magistrate comming
towardes them, (as being called back by the Common-weale
for more serious imployments) or doe but heare that hee
lyes sicke, vpon whom the health of a Cittie is put in hazard:
they presently (like Prentises vpon *Shoue-tuesday*) take the
lawe in their owne handes, and doe what they list. And this
Legion consists of Market-folkes, Bakers, Brewers, all that
weigh their Consciences in Scales. And lastly, of the two
degrees of Colliers, *viz.* those of Char-coles, and those of
New-castle. Then haue you the *Shauing* of Fatherlesse
children, and of widowes, and thats done by Executors.
The *Shauing* of poore Clients especially by the Atturneyes
Clearkes of your Courts, and thats done by writing their
Billes of costs vpon *Cheuerell*. The *Shauing* of prisoners by
extortion, first, taken by their keepers, for a prison is builded
on such ranke and fertil ground, that if poore wretches sow it
with hand-fulles of small debts when they come in, if they lie
there but a while to see the comming vp of them : the charges
of the house will bee treble the demaund of the Creditor.
Then haue you *Brokers* yat *shaue* poore men by most
iewish interest : marry the diuils trimme them so soone
as they haue washed others. I wil not tell how Vintners
shaue their Guestes with a little peece of Paper not
aboue three fingers broade ; for their roomes are like Barbars
Chaires : Men come into them willingly to bee *Shauen*. Onely
(which is worst) bee it knowne to thee (*O thou Queene of Cities*)
thy Inhabitants *Shaue* their *Consciences* so close, that in the
ende they growe balde, and bring foorth no goodnesse.

Wee haue beene quicke (you see) in *Trimming* this *Cutter* of
QueeneHith, because tis his propertie to handle others so, let
vs bee as nymble in praysing his *Household-stuffe* : The best
part of which is his *Chariot*, richly adorned, It is drawen by
foure beasts : the 2. formost are a *Wolfe* (which will eate till he
be readie to burst) and hee is Coach-fellow to a *she-Beare*,

who is cruell euen to women great with childe : behinde
them are a couple of *Blood-houndes* : the Coach-man is as
Informer. Two *Pettifoggers* that haue beene turned ouer
the barre, are his Lackies ; his *Houshold seruants* are *Wit*
(who is his Steward) *Audacitie*: *Shifting* : *Inexorabilitie* : and
Disquietnesse of mind : The Meanie are (besides some persons
before named) skeldring soldiers, and begging schollers.

Crueltie;

Or

The seuenth and last dayes Triumph.

What a weeke of sinfull *Reueling* hath heere bin with these *six* proud Lords of Misrule? to which of your *Hundred* parishes (O you *Citizens*) haue not some one of these (if not all) remoued their Courts and feasted you with them? your Percullises are not strong inough to keepe them out by day your Watchmen are too sleepy to spie their stealing in by night. ·There is yet another to enter, as great in power as his fellowes, as subtill, as full of mis-chiefe: If I shoulde name him to you, you would laugh mee to scorne, because you cannot bee perswaded that such a one should euer bee suffered to liue within the freedome: yet if I name him not to you, you may in time, by him (as by the rest) bee vndone. It is *Crueltie*, O strange! me thinkes *London* should start vp out of her sollid foundation, and in anger bee ready to fall vppon him, and grinde him to dust that durst say, shee is possest with such a deuill. *Cruelty!* the verie sound of it shewes that it is no English word: it is a *Fury* sent out of hel, not to inhabit within such beautifull walles, but amongst Turkes and Tartars. The other sixe Monsters transforme themselues into Amiable shapes, and set golden, inticing Charmes to winne men to their *Circæan* loue, they haue *Angelical* faces to allure, and bewitching tongues to inchaunt: But *Cruelty* is a hag, horred in forme, terrible ·in voice, formidable in threates, A tyrant in his very lookes, and a murderer in all his actions.

How then commeth it to passe that heere he seekes entertainment? For what Cittie in the world, does more drie vp
the teares of the Widdowe, and giues more warmth to the
fatherlesse then this ancient and reuerend *Grandam* of Citties?
Where hath the *Orphan* (that is to receiue great portions)
lesse cause to mourne the losse of Parents? He findes foure
and twentie graue *Senators* to his Fathers instead of one:
the Cittie it selfe to bee his Mother; her Officers to bee his
Seruants, who see that hee want nothing: her lawes to suffer
none to doe him wrong: and though he be neuer so simple
in wit, or so tender in yeares, shee lookes as warily to that
welth which is left him, as to the Apple of her owne eye.
Where haue the Leaper and the Lunatick Surgery, and
Phisicke so good cheape as heere? their payment is onely
thankes: large Hospitalls are erected (of purpose to make
them lodgings) and the rent is most easie, onely their prayers:
yet for all this, that Charitie hath her Armes full of children,
and that tender-brested Compassion is still in one street or
other dooing good workes: off from the Hindges are one of the
7. *Gates* readie to bee lifted, to make roome for this Giant:
the Whiflers of your inferior and Chiefe companies cleere
the wayes before him, men of all trades with shoutes and
acclamations followed in thronges behinde him, yea euen the
siluer-bearded, and seuearest lookt cittizens haue giuen him
welcomes in their Parlors.

· There are in Lond[on], and within the buildings, yat round
about touch her sides, and stand within her reach, *Thirteene
strong houses of sorrow*, where the prisoners hath his heart
wasting away sometimes a whole prentiship of yeres in cares.
They are most of them built of Freestone, but none are free
within them: cold are their imbracements: vnwholsom[e] is
their cheare: dispaireful their lodgings, vncomfortable their
societies, miserable their inhabitants: O what a deale of
wretchednes can make shift to lye in a little roome! if those
13 houses were built al together, how rich wold Griefe be,
hauing such large inclosures? Doth cruelty challenge a
freemans roome in the City because of these places? no, the
politicke body of the Republike wold be infected, if such
houses as these were not maintained, to keepe vp those that
are vnsound. Claimes he then an inheritance here, because
you haue whipping postes in your streete for the Vagabond?

the Stocks and the cage for the vnruely beggar? or because you haue Carts for the Bawde and the Harlot, and Beadles for the Lecher? neither.   Or is it because so many monthly Sessions are held? so many men, women and Children cald to a reconing at the Bar of death for their liues? and so many lamentable hempen Tragedies acted at *Tiburne*? nor for this : *Iustice* should haue wrong, to haue it so. reported.   No (you Inhabitants of this little world of people) Crueltie is a large Tree and you all stand vnder it : you are cruel in *Against forced Mariages.*   compelling your children (for wealth) to goe into loathed beds, for therby you make them bond-slaues : what ploughman is so foolish to yoake young hecfars and old bullocks together? yet such is your husbandry.   In fitting your Coaches with horses, you are very curious to haue them (so neere as you can) both of a colour, both of a height, of an age, of proportion, and will you bee carelesse in coupling your Children? he into whose bosome threescore winters haue thrust their frozen fingars, if hee be rich (though his breath bee rancker then a Muck-hill, his bodye more drye than *Mummi*, and his minde more lame than *Ignorance* it selfe) shall haue offered vnto him (but it is offered as a sacrifice) the tender bossome of a Virgin, vpon whose fore-head was neuer written sixteene yeares : if she refuse this liuing death (for lesse than a death it cannot be vnto her) She is threatned to bee left an out-cast, cursd for disobedience, raild at daily, and reuylde howerlye : to saue herselfe from which basenes, She desp[e]rately runnes into a bondage, and goes to Church to bee married, as if she went to be buried.   But what glorye atcheiue you in these conquests? you doe wrong to Time, inforcing May to embrace December : you dishonour Age, in bringing it into scorne for insufficiency, into a loathing for dotage, into all mens laughter for iealousie.   You made your Daughters looke wrinckled with sorrowes, before they be olde, and your sonnes by riot, to be beggars in midst of their youth. Hences come it, yat murders are often contriued, and as often acted : our countrie is woful in fresh examples : Hence comes it, yat the Courtiers giues you an open scoffe, ye clown a secret mock, the Cittizen yat dwels at your thres-hald, a ieery frump : Hence it is yat if you goe by water in the calmest day, you are driuen by some fatall storme.

into ye vnlucky and dangerous hauen betweene *Greenewich* and *London.* You haue another cruelty in keeping men in prison so long, til sicknes and death deal mildely *Against* with them, and (in despite of al tyranny) baile *cruell Creditors.* them out of all executions. When you see a poore wretch that to keep life in a loathed body hath not a house left to couer his head from the tempestes, nor a bed (but the common bedde which our Mother the earth allowes him) for his cares to sleepe vppon, when you haue (by keeping or locking him vp) robd him of all meanes to get, what seeke you to haue him loose but his life ? The miserable prisoner is ready to famish, yet that cannot mooue you, the more miserable wife is readye to runne mad with despaire, yet that cannot melt you: the moste of all miserable, his Children lye crying at your dores, yet nothing can awaken in you compassion : if his debts be heauie, the greater and more glorious is your pitty to worke his freedome, if they be light, the sharper is the *Vengeance* that will be heaped vpon your heades for your hardenes of heart Wee are moste like to God that made vs, when wee shew loue one to another, and doe moste looke like the Diuell that would destroy vs, when wee are one anothers tormenters. If any haue so much flint growing about his bosome, that he will needes make Dice of mens bones, I would there were a lawe to compell him to make drinking bowles of their Sculs too: and that euerie miserable debter that so dyes, might be buried at his Creditors doore, that when hee strides ouer him he might thinke he still rises vp (like the Ghost in *Ieronimo*) crying *Reuenge.*

Crueltie hath yet another part to play, it is acted (like the old Morralls at *Maningtree*) by Trades-men, marrye *Against* seuerall companies in the Citie haue it in study, and *vnconsionable Maisters* they are neuer perfect in it, till the end of seauen yeares at least, at which time, they come off with it roundly And this it is : When your seruants haue made themselues bondmen to inioy your fruitefull hand-maides, thats to say, to haue an honest and thriuing Art to liue by : when they haue fared hardly with you by Indenture, and like your Beasts which carry you haue patiently borne al labours, and all wrongs you could lay vpon them.

When you haue gathered the blossomes of their youth, and reaped the fruites of her strength, And that you can no longer (for shame) hold them in Captiuitie, but that by the lawes of your Country and of conscience you must vndoe their fetters, Then, euen then doe you hang moste weightes at their heeles, to make them sincke downe for euer: when you are bound to send them into the world to liue, you send them into the world to beg: they seru'd you seuen yeeres to pick vp a poore liuing, and therein you are iust, for you will be sure it shall be a poore liuing indeede they shall pick vp: for what do the rich cubs? like foxes they lay their heads together in conspiracy, burying their leaden consciences vnder the earth, to the intent that all waters that are wholesome in taste, and haue the sweetnes of gaine in going downe, may be drawne through them only, being the great pipes of their Company, because they see tis the custome of the Citty, to haue all waters that come thither, conueyed by such large vessels, and they will not breake the customes of the Citty. When they haue the fulnesse of welth to the brim, that it runs ouer, they scarce will suffer their poore Seruant to take that which runs at waste, nor to gather vp the wind-fals, when all the great trees, as if they grew in the garden of the *Hesperides*, are laden with golden apples: no, they would not haue them gleane the scattered eares of corne, though they themselues cary away ye full sheafes; as if Trades that were ordained to the *Communities*, had lost their first priuiledges, and were now turnd to *Monopolyes*. But remember (ô you *Rich men*) that your Seruants are your adopted Children, they are naturalized into your bloud, and if you hurt theirs, you are guilty of letting out your owne, than which, what *Cruelty* can be greater?

What *Gallenist* or *Paracelsian* in the world, by all his water-casting, and minerall extractions, would iudge, that this fairest-fac'de daughter of *Brute*, (and good daughter to King *Lud*, who gaue her her name) should haue so much *2700 and odde yeeres since London was first builded by Brute.* corruption in her body? vnlesse (that beeing now two thousand and seuen hundred yeeres old) extreme age should fill her full of diseases! Who durst not haue sworne for her, that of all loathsome sinnes that euer bred within her, she had neuer toucht the sinne of cruelty? It had wont to be a Spanish *Sicknes*, and hang long (incurably) vpon the body of their Inquisition; or else a French disease, running all ouer that Kingdome in a *Massacre*;

. but that it had infected the English, especially the people of this now once-againe *New-reard-Troy*, it was beyond beliefe. But is she cleerely purg'd of it by those pills that haue before bin giuen her? Is she now sound? Are there no dregs of this thick and pestilenciall poyson, eating still through her bowels? Yes: the vgliest Serpent hath not vncurld himselfe. She hath sharper and more black inuenomed stings within her, than yet haue bin shot forth.

There is a *Cruelty* within thee (faire *Troynouant*) worse and more barbarous then all the rest, because it is *Against want of places for Buriall in Dead Sonnes and Daughters.* Against thy dead *extremity of sicknes.* children wert thou cruell in that dreadfull, horrid, and *Tragicall* yeere, when 30000 of them (struck with 1602. plagues from heauen) dropt downe in winding-sheets at thy feet. Thou didst then take away all *Ceremonies* due vnto them, and haledst them rudely to their last beds (like drunkards) without the dead mans musick (his *Bell.*) Alack, this was nothing: but thou tumbledst them into their euerlasting lodgings (ten in one heape, and twenty in another) as if all the roomes vpon earth had bin full. The gallant and the begger lay together; the scholler and the carter in one bed: the husband saw his wife, and his deadly enemy whom he hated, within a paire of sheetes. Sad and vnsemely are such *Funeralls*: So felons that are cut downe from the tree of shame and dishonor, are couered in the earth: So souldiers, after a mercilesse battaile, receiue vnhan[d]some buriall. But suppose the *Pestiferous Deluge* should againe drowne this little world of thine, and that thou must be compeld to breake open those caues of horror and gastlinesse, to hide more of thy dead houshold in them, what rotten stenches, and contagious damps would strike vp into thy nosthrils? thou couldst not lift vp thy head into the aire, for that (with her condensed sinnes) would stifle thee, thou couldst not diue into the waters, for that they being teinted by the ayre, would poison thee. Art thou now not cruell against thy selfe, in not prouiding (before the land-waters of *Affliction* come downe againe vpon thee) more and more conuenient Cabins to lay those in, that are to goe into such farre countries, who neuer looke to come back againe? If thou shouldst deny it, the Graues when they open, will be witnesses against thee.

Nay, thou hast yet *Another Cruelty* gnawing in thy bosome ;
Against want of prouision for those that dye in the fields. for what hope is there yat thou shouldst haue pitty ouer others, when thou art vnmercifull to thy self! Looke ouer thy walls into thy Orchards and Gardens, and thou shalt see thy seruants and apprentises sent out cunningly by their Masters at noone day vpon deadly errands, when they perceiue that the *Armed Man* hath struck them, yea euen when they see they haue tokens deliuered them from heauen to hasten thither, then send they them forth to walke vpon their graues, and to gather the flowers themselues that shall stick their own Herse. And this thy Inhabitants do, because they are loth and ashamed to haue a writing ouer their dores, to tell that God hath bin there, they had rather all their enemies in the world put them to trouble, then that he should visit them.

Looke againe ouer the walls into thy Fields, and thou shalt heare poore and forsaken wretches lye groaning in ditches, and trauailing to seeke out Death vpon thy common hye wayes. Hauing found him, he there throwes downe their infected carcases, towards which, all that passe by, looke, but (till common shame, and common necessity compell) none step in to giue them buriall. Thou setst vp posts to whip them when they are aliue : Set vp an Hospitall to comfort them being sick, or purchase ground for them to dwell in when they be well, and that is, when they be dead.

Is it not now hye time to sound a *Retreate*, after so terrible
The Conclusion. a battaile fought betweene the seuen *Electors* of the *Low Infernall Countryes*, and one little City? What armyes come marching along with them? What bloudy cullors do they spread? What Artillery do they mount to batter the walls? How valiant are their seuen *Generalls*? How expert? How full of fortune to conquer? Yet nothing sooner ouerthrowes them, than to bid them battaile first, and to giue them defiance.

Who can denye now, but that *Sinne* (like the seuen-headed *Nylus*) hath ouerflowed thy banks and thy buildings (*o* thu glory of *Great Brittaine*) and made thee fertile (for many yeeres together) in all kindes of *Vices*? *Volga*, that hath fifty streames falling one into another, neuer ranne with so swift and vnres[i]stable a current as these *Black-waters* do, to bring vpon thee an *Inundation.*

If thou (as thou hast done) kneelest to worship this *Beast* with *Seuen Crowned Heads*, and the *Whore* that sits vpon it, the fall of thee (thou hast out-stood so many Citties) will be greater then that of *Babylon.* She is now gotten within thy walls ; she rides vp and downe thy streetes, making thee drunke out of her cup, and marking thee in the forhead with pestilence for her owne. She causes *Violls* of wrath to be powred vpon thee, and goes in triumph away, when she sees thee falling. If thou wilt be safe therefore and recouer health, rise vp in Armes against her, and driue her (and the *Monster* that beares her) out at thy *Gates.* Thou seest how prowdly and impetuously sixe of these *Centuares* (that are halfe man, halfe beast, and halfe diuell) come thundring alongst thy Habitations, and what rabbles they bring at their heeles ; take now but note of the last, and marke how the seuenth rides : for if thou findest but the least worthy quality in any one of them to make thee loue him, I will write a *Retractation* of what is inueyd against them before, and pollish such an *Apology* in their defence, that thou shalt be enamored of them all.

The body and face of this *Tyrannous Commander*, that leades thus the *Reareward*, are already drawne : his Chariot is framed all of ragged *Flint* so artificially bestowed, that as it runnes, they strike one another, and beate out fire that is able to consume Citties : the wheeles are many, and swift : the Spokes of the wheeles, are the Shinbones of wretches that haue bin eaten by misery out of prison. A couple of vnruly, fierce, and vntamed Tygers (cald *Murder* and *Rashnes*) drew the Chariot : *Ignorance* holds the reynes of the one, and *Obduration* of the other : *Selfe-will* is the *Coachman.* In the vpper end of the *Coach*, sits *Cruelty* alone, vpon a bench made of dead mens sculls. All the way that he rides, he sucks the hearts of widdowes and father-lesse children. He keepes neither foote-men nor Pages, for none will stay long with him. He hath onely one attendant that euer followes him, called *Repentance*, but the Beast that drawes him, runnes away with his good Lord and Master so fast before, that *Repentance* being lame (and therefore slow) tis alwayes very late ere he comes to him. It is to be feared, that *Cruelty* is of

great authority where he is knowne, for few or none dare
stand against him : *Law* only now and then beards him, and
stayes him, in contempt of those that so terribly gallop before
him ; but out of the Lawes hands, if he can but snatch a
sheathed sword (as oftentimes hee does) presently hee whips it
out, smiting and wounding with it euery one that giues him
the least crosse word. He comes into the Citty, commonly at
All-gate, beeing drawne that way by the smell of bloud about
the Barres, (for by his good will he drinks no other liquor :)
but when ·hee findes it to be the bloud of Beasts (amongst
the Butchers) and not of men, he flyes like lightning along
the Causey in a madnes, threatning to ouer-runne all whom
he meetes: but spying the Brokers of *Hownsditch* shuffling
themselues so long together (like a false paire of Cards) till
the Knaues be vppermost, onely to doe homage to him, he stops,
kissing all their cheekes, calling them all his deerest Sonnes ;
and bestowing a damnable deale of his blessing
vpon them, they cry, *Roome* for *Cruelty,*
and are the onely men that bring
him into the Citty:
To follow whom vp and downe so farre
as they meane to goe with him,

—Dii me terrent, et Iupiter hostis.

FINIS.

Tho. Dekker.